P9-COP-400

snapshot·picture·library

HORSES

snapshot·picture·library

HORSES

FOG CITY PRESS

Published by Fog City Press,
a division of Weldon Owen Inc.
415 Jackson Street
San Francisco, CA 94111
www.weldonowen.com

WELDON OWEN GROUP
Chief Executive Officer John Owen
Chief Financial Officer Simon Fraser

WELDON OWEN INC.
President, Chief Executive Officer Terry Newell
Vice President, International Sales Stuart Laurence
Vice President, Sales and New Business Development Amy Kaneko
Vice President, Sales—Asia and Latin America Dawn Low
Vice President, Publisher Roger Shaw
Vice President, Creative Director Gaye Allen
Managing Editor, Fog City Press Karen Perez
Assistant Editor Sonia Vallabh
Art Director Kelly Booth
Designer Andreas Schueller
Design Assistant Justin Hallman
Production Director Chris Hemesath
Production Manager Michelle Duggan
Sales Manager Emily Bartle
Color Manager Teri Bell

Text Nancy Wilson Hall
Picture Research Andy Sir

A WELDON OWEN PRODUCTION
© 2007 Weldon Owen Inc.

All rights reserved, including the right
of reproduction in whole or in part in any form.

Library of Congress Control Number: 2007936040

ISBN-13: 978-1-74089-641-2
ISBN-10: 1-74089-641-6

10 9 8 7 6 5 4 3 2

Color separations by Sang Choy International, Singapore.
Printed by Tien Wah Press in Singapore.

People and horses work and
play together all over the world.

We take care of horses. Horses
carry us on their strong backs
and help us with our work.

These beautiful animals have
become our very good friends.
Have you ever seen horses
like the ones in this book?

Baby horses
are called foals.
At first, foals
like to stay
close to their
mothers. But
soon they learn
to run and play
on their own.

A father horse is
called a stallion.
Stallions look
after all the horses
in the herd.

Even though they are very large,
most horses are gentle and friendly.

A horse may
have a best
friend—just
like people do.

Horses live all over the world. Some live in warm places…

But they are happy in cold places,
too. In the winter their coats
grow thick to keep them warm.

A curious horse's
ears stand tall
and face forward.

Alert ears and a high tail
show that a horse is happy.

A blaze is a white stripe on the face.
White legs are called stockings.

Boy horses are called colts when they are young and stallions when they grow up.

A young girl horse is called a filly. She is called a mare when she grows up.

These working
horses help
cowboys to
move cows
on ranches.

Other horses
live and work
on farms.

These horses are all saddled up.
Would you like to go for a ride?

Show horses
have their
manes and
tails brushed
and braided.

Wild horses live
on their own on
the prairie…

...or in the mountains. But
everywhere they go, horses
like to nibble on tasty grass.

Very small horses are called ponies.

A foal needs
plenty of
rest—just
like you do.

Grown-up horses like
to relax in the pasture.

When horses
play, they kick
their legs high
into the air.

Horses love to gallop on
their long, graceful legs.

Their manes
and tails flow
in the wind.

A strong sense of smell and
good eyesight help horses
to learn about the world.

A horse needs
lots of care.

Clean water and
lots of grass to
eat help to keep
a horse healthy.

Fences keep them
from getting lost.

So that they can be
friends with you!

ACKNOWLEDGMENTS

Weldon Owen would like to thank
the following people for their
assistance in the production of this
book: Diana Heom, Ashley Martinez,
Danielle Parker, Lucie Parker,
Phil Paulick, and Erin Zaunbrecher.

CREDITS

Key t=top; b=bottom; DT=Dreamstime;
iSP=iStockphoto; LO=Lucky Oliver;
SST=Shutterstock

2 SST; 5 SST; 6 iSP; 8 DT; 9t iSP, b iSP;
11 SST; 12 SST; 13 iSP; 14 SST; 15t DT,
b iSP; 17 SST; 18 SST; 19 SST; 20 SST;
22 SST; 23 SST; 24 DT; 25 DT; 26t DT,
b iSP; 27 DT; 28 SST; 30 SST; 31t DT, b iSP;
32t DT, b iSP; 33 DT; 34 DT; 35 SST; 36 SST;
37t DT, b iSP; 38 SST; 40 DT; 41 SST; 42 iSP;
43 DT; 45 SST; 46 iSP; 47 SST; 48t iSP, b SST;
49 SST; 50 SST; 51 SST; 52 SST; 54 DT;
55 SST; 57 DT; 58t DT, b SST; 59 DT; 60 SST;
62 SST; 63 SST; 64 DT.